LIVES AND TIMES

Florence Nightingale

Rebecca Vickers

Heinemann Library
Chicago, Illinois

Customer Service 888-454-2279

Visit our website at www.heinemannlibrary.com

Designed by Visual Image
Illustrations by Sally Barton
Originated by Dot Gradations
Printed and bound in Hong Kong/China

06 05 04 03 02
10 9 8 7 6 5 4 3 2

Library of Congress Cataloging-in-Publication Data
Vickers, Rebecca.
    Florence Nightingale / Rebecca Vickers.
            p. cm. -- (Lives and times)
    Includes bibliographical references and index.
    Summary: A simple introduction to the life and work of Florence Nightingale, the nineteenth-century English woman considered to be the founder of modern nursing.
    ISBN 1-57572-402-2 (lib. bdg.)   ISBN 1-4034-0028-8 (pbk. bdg.)
    1. Nightingale, Florence, 1820-1910--Juvenile literature. 2.
Nurses--England--Biography--Juvenile literature. [1. Nightingale, Florence, 1820-1910.
2. Nurses. 3. Women--Biography.] I. Title. II. Lives and times (Des Plaines, Ill.)

RT37.N5 V53 2000
610.73'092--dc21
    [B]   00-035021

Acknowledgments
The Publishers would like to thank the following for permission to reproduce photographs: Eye Ubiquitous: G. Daniels p.17; Hulton Getty: p.16; Peter Newark's Historical Pictures: p.18; Florence Nightingale Museum: pp.19, 20, 21, 22, 23.
Cover photograph reproduced with permission of Hulton Getty.

Every effort has been made to contact copyright holders of any material reproduced in this book. Any omissions will be rectified in subsequent printings if notice is given to the publisher.

Some words are shown in bold, **like this.** You can find out what they mean by looking in the glossary.

Contents

Part One

Florence Nightingale was born in 1820. Her parents were visiting Florence, in Italy. She was named after the city. Florence had an older sister named Parthenope.

Florence's parents were very rich. Like many girls of the time, Florence did not go to school. But she was a good student. Her father taught her foreign languages, history, and math.

Florence's childhood was happy. As she grew older, Florence's parents thought she should find a rich young man and settle down as a wife and mother. This was what girls her age were expected to do.

Florence realized that she wanted to nurse the sick. At the time, nurses were often **uneducated** old women. They were nothing like Florence. Her parents would not let her be a nurse.

Florence read books and reports about health and hospitals. She became an **expert** on ways to keep people healthy and make them better when they became sick. She was sure that she wanted to be a nurse and help people.

When she was 26, Florence went to Germany with some friends. She visited a nursing school in Kaiserswerth. This was where she wanted to study!

In 1851, Florence's parents let her go to Kaiserswerth. Then she went to Paris, France, to work as a nurse. Later she worked at a hospital for sick women in London.

In 1854, Nightingale heard about the bad conditions for soldiers injured in the **Crimean War** between Britain and Russia. She knew she had to help.

Nightingale gathered together supplies and a group of nurses. They traveled to Scutari Hospital in Turkey. Most of the injured soldiers were sent to Scutari. They had unhealthy food. There were no beds.

The men were happy to have cleaner **wards** and better food. They called Nightingale "The Lady with the Lamp" because she walked around the hospital every night comforting patients.

When the war ended in 1856, Nightingale was famous. Even Queen Victoria wanted to meet her. Everyone wanted Nightingale's advice about hospitals and health. In 1860, she set up the Nightingale School for Nurses in London.

Nightingale became very sick. She spent most of her time at home, but people came to ask her for advice about hospitals. She died in 1910. During her life nursing had become a respected **profession**.

Part Two

Two hundred years ago there were no educated nurses to look after sick and injured people. Hospitals were often crowded, noisy, and dirty places.

Today patients in hospitals are looked after by trained nurses. One reason for this is the hard work and **dedication** of Florence Nightingale.

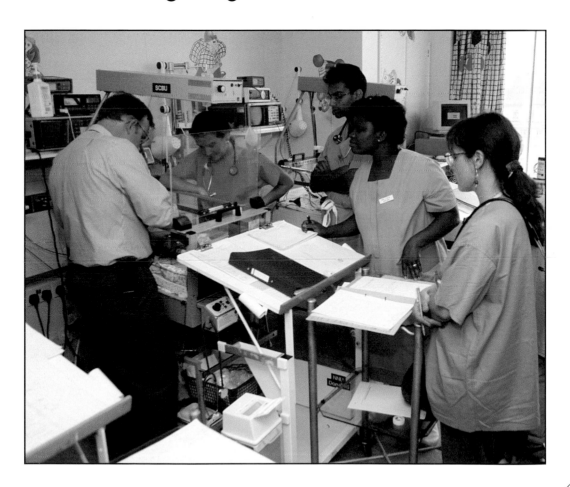

We can find out more about Nightingale by looking at pictures. This painting is a watercolor of Florence and Parthenope when they were young. Florence is sewing, so she is looking down.

Here is a painting of Nightingale when she was about 35 years old. She is in a **ward** of the Barracks Hospital in Scutari.

Here is Nightingale with a group of nurses from the Nightingale School for Nurses at St. Thomas's Hospital in London. At the Nightingale School nurses learned by helping in a hospital. This had never happened before.

Nightingale was blind for the last ten years of her life. She was sick for a long time, but she kept working until she lost her sight. This photograph shows her writing letters.

In London there is a Florence Nightingale Museum. It contains **artifacts** from Nightingale's life. Here are her pen, ink bottle, watch, and writing box.

This is the lamp that Nightingale used to visit the sick soldiers in the hospital **wards**. She did this in Scutari during the **Crimean War**.

Glossary

artifact thing that people make and use that helps us learn about the past
You say *art-uh-fact.*

Crimean War (1854–1856) fought in an area on the Black Sea, in the southeast of what is now the Ukraine
You say *cry-me-un.*

dedication doing something with total love and devotion

expert someone who knows a lot about a subject

profession job with special school or tests to pass before you can do it

uneducated someone who has not been to school

ward large, open room with many beds, found in hospitals

Index

More Books to Read

Children's Press. *Florence Nightingale.* Danbury, Conn.: Children's Press, 1991.

Davis, Lucille. *Florence Nightingale.* Mankato, Minn.: Capstone Press, 1999.

Shore, Donna, and Giani Renna. *Florence Nightingale.* Parsippany, N.J.: Silver Burdett Press, 1990.

24